ᓴᓂᕋᔭᒃ, ᑲᔾᔮᕆᔭᕋ

Sanirajak, a Place I Love

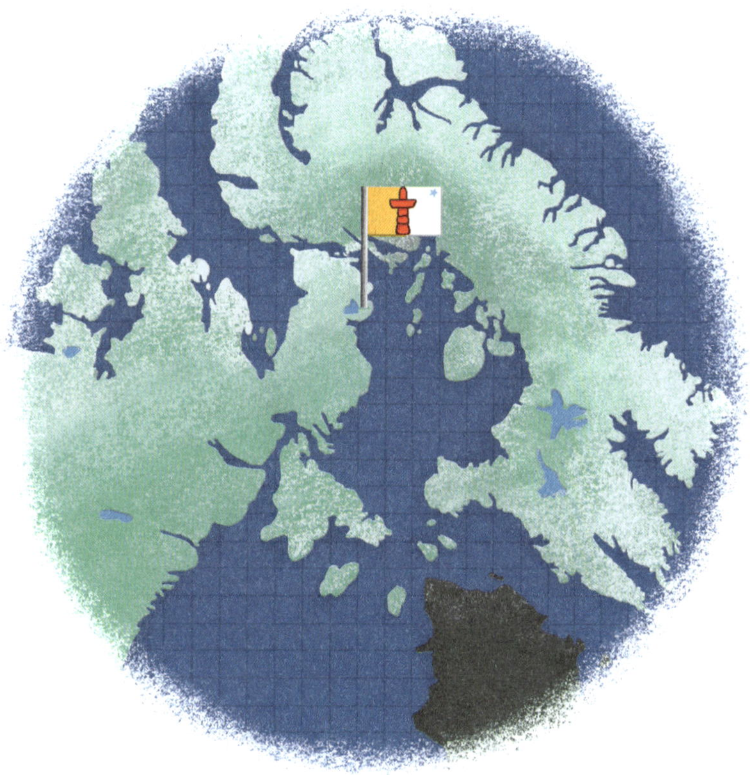

ᑎᑎᕋᖅᑐᖅ
ᐋᓚᔅ ᖃᓈᑦᓯᐊᖅ
ᑎᑎᖅᑐᒐᖅᑐᖅ
ᔫᓕᐊ ᑲᓚᑕ

WRITTEN BY
Alice Qanatsiaq
ILLUSTRATED BY
Julia Galotta

ᐋᓚᔅᖑᔪᖓ, ᓴᓂᕋᔭᖕᒥᐅᑕᐅᔪᖓ, ᓄᓇᕗᒻᒥ.
ᑲᔾᔮᓇᔭᕙᔾᔪᐊᕿᓗᒐ.

My name is Alice, and I live in Sanirajak, Nunavut.
It is a place I love so much.

ᓴᓂᕋᔭᒃ ᑲᔾᔪᓇᔭᕋ ᐅᐱᕐᖔᒃᑯᑦ. ᓯᓚ ᐅᖅᑰᓯᕙᓪᓕᐊᕙᖕᒪᑦ
ᐅᖅᑰᓯᕙᓪᓕᐊᑐᐃᓐᓇᖅᓱᓂ, ᓯᕿᓐᓂᑯᑖᓕᖅᐸᓪᓕᐊᕙᒻᒪᑦ.
ᐅᓐᓄᒃᑯᑦ ᓯᓚ, ᓂᓪᓚᓱᒃᑐᐊᓘᕙᒃᑑᒐᓗᐊᖅ.

I love Sanirajak in the spring. The weather gets warmer and warmer, and the sun is out for longer and longer. It is still very cold at night, though.

ᐊᐅᓚᓴᕆᐊᖕᒪ ᖁᕕᐊᒋᔭᕋ. ᐱᓇᓱᐊᕈᓱᐅᑉ ᓄᖖᒧᖕᒪ ᑎᑭᑦᑕᐅᑎᒋᖅᑲᑦᑕᙱᓗᐊᖅᑐᖅ ᐃᖅᑲᓪᓚᐊᕈᒪᓪᓗᓂ!

ᓄᓇᖅᑲᑎᒌᑦ ᐃᖅᑲᓗᒐᓱᒋᐊᓲᑦ ᑕᓯᐅᔭᕐᒧᑦ, ᑕᓯᕐᔪᐊᕌᓗᒃ. ᐃᓄᐃᑦ ᐅᐸᒪᓐᓈᖅᑲᓲᖑᕗᑦ ᐊᔾᔨᒌᙱᑦᑐᓂᒃ ᐃᖅᑲᓪᓚᐊᖅᕕᖕᒋᓐᓂᒃ.

ᑕᓯᐅᔭᖅ ᐃᖢᕋᖅᑲᖅᑐᖅ ᑕᓇᐅᖅᒥᐅᑕᖅᑲᖅᖢᓂᓗ. ᓯᑯᖕᒪ ᑕᐅᕙᓂ ᐃᔾᔪᔪᐊᓗᒃ! ᐊᖑᑏᑦ ᐃᑰᑕᓲᑦ ᐊᒃᓱᕈᖅᖢᑎᒃ ᐃᖅᑲᓗᒐᓱᖕᓂᐊᕋᑦᑕ.

I love ice fishing. I am always excited when the weekend comes. It means we get to go fishing!

People in my community like to fish at Tasiujaq, which is a big lake. Everyone has different spots where they like to fish.

Tasiujaq has trout and char. The ice here is very thick! The men work hard to drill holes so that we can fish.

ᐃᖃᓗᓚᓯᑎᐊᖓ ᖁᕕᐊᓇᕐᓂᖅᐹᖑᓲᖑᕗᖅ ᑎᖕᒥᐊᑦ ᐅᑎᐊᓕᖅᑎᑦᓱᑎᑦ. ᑕᓯᕐᒦᔅᓱᖓ, ᑐᓴᓲᒃᑲ ᑲᖑᐃᑦ ᓂᕐᓖᑦᑐ ᖁᓕᓐᓂᑦ. ᑲᔾᔮᕐᓇᖅᑐᐊᓗᒃ ᓴᐃᓕᓇᖅᓱᓂᓗ.

ᖁᕕᐊᑎᓛᓐᓂᑦᑕᐅᖅ ᐊᐅᓪᓛᖅᓯᒪᓪᓗᓂ ᐱᓕᕆᓲᖑᕗᒍᑦ: ᐱᑭᐅᑕᖅ.

The best time to fish is when the birds come back in the spring, after they have spent the winter in the south. When I'm out on the lake, I can hear the snow geese and Canada geese honking above me. It is so beautiful and calming.

It also makes me excited for my other favourite thing to do on the land: collecting eggs.

ᐃᓚᒌᕐᓗᑕ ᖁᑭᖅᑕᒨᕈᒪᓲᖑᔪᒍᑦ ᓴᓂᕋᔭᐅᑉ ᖃᓂᒋᔮᓂᑦ ᐱᑭᐅᑕᓇᐊᖅᓗᑕ.
ᐊᔾᔨᒌᙱᑦᑐᐊᓗᖕᓂᒃ ᐱᑭᐅᑕᖅᓇᖅᑐᖅ ᓄᓇᖓ.

ᑎᑭᑦᑕᕌᖓᑦᑕ, ᖃᑦᑕᒡᒋᖅᓗᑕ ᐱᓱᖁᔭᓕᖅᐸᒃᑐᒍᑦ. ᓯᕗᓪᓕᖅᒥ,
ᑐᐊᕕᖅᓗᖓ ᒪᓐᓂᒃᓯᐅᖅᐸᒃᑐᖓ! ᐊᑯᓂᐅᙱᑦᑐᖅ, ᐃᖅᑲᐃᓲᖑᔪᖓ
ᓱᒃᑲᐃᔾᔫᒥᔭᓇᐊᖅᑲᖅᓂᓐᓂᑦ. ᑲᔾᔮᕈᓱᖕᓂᐊᖃᒪ ᐃᓚᓐᓂᒃ ᐱᖃᓐᓇᕆᔭᓐᓂᓪᓗ
ᐱᖃᑎᖃᕐᓗᖓ.

My family likes to go to the islands near Sanirajak to pick eggs. There are all sorts of bird eggs to find out on the land.

When we arrive, I start rushing around looking for eggs. But after a while, I remember to slow down. I want to enjoy being out on the land with my family and friends.

ᐊᐅᓯᐃᑦ ᓴᓂᕋᔭᖕᒥ ᑲᔫᕐᓇᕐᓂᖅᓴᒻᒪᕆᐊᓘᕗᑦ. ᖃᐅᒪᐃᓐᓇᖃᑦᑕᓕᖅᑎᓪᓗᒍ ᐅᓪᓗᒃᑯᑦ ᐅᓐᓄᐊᒃᑯᓪᓗ. ᓯᓚ ᑲᔫᕐᓇᑦᑎᐊᖅᐸᓂ ᐅᖅᑰᓪᓗᓂᓗ, ᐃᓄᓕᒫᑦᑎᐊᓪᓗ ᐊᓃᓕᖅᐸᑎᒃ! ᐊᐅᔭᒃᑯᑦ ᖃᓄᐃᓕᐅᒐᒃᓴᖅᑕᕐᑲᐃᓐᓇᕌᖕᒍᕗᖅ.

ᐃᓄᓕᒫᐸᓗᐃᑦ ᐊᐅᓪᓛᖅᓯᒪᓕᖃᑦᑕᕐᒪᑕ. ᖁᕕᐊᓇᖅᑐᐊᓘᖕᒪᑦ ᐊᐅᓪᓛᖅᓯᒪᓪᓗᓂ ᓄᓇᓖᑦ ᓯᓚᑖᓄᑦ.

Summers in Sanirajak are even better than spring. It is light out all day and all night. The weather is nice and warm, and almost everyone is outside! There are always things to do in summer.

A lot of people love to go out on the land. It is so much fun to travel outside the community!

ᑲᔾᔫᕐᓇᖅᑐᐊᓘᒋᕗᖅ ᐊᖑᓇᓱᒃᑏᑦ ᐊᐃᕝᕙᖃᑦᑕᓕᖅᑎᓪᓗᒋᑦ.
ᐊᐃᕚᑦ ᐊᖏᔪᕙᔾᔪᐊᖄᓗᐃᕐ!

ᐊᐃᕚᑦ ᐃᒍᓇᖅᓯᐊᖑᓲᖑᕗᑦ, ᐅᑭᐅᒃᑯᑦ ᓂᕿᑦᑎᐊᕚᓗᐃᑦ.
ᓄᓇᓖᑦ ᓴᓇᕿᔭᐅᑉ ᓯᓚᑖᓂᒥᐅᑦ ᑎᑭᓴᐃᓲᑦ ᐃᒍᓇᕐᓂᒃ.

It is nice when hunters start to catch walruses.
Walruses are really big!

Walrus meat is made into *igunaq**, which is saved to eat in the winter. People from other communities order igunaq from Sanirajak.

***igunaq** (EE-goo-nak): Igunaq is walrus meat that is prepared like a bundle or a sack, with the meat put inside the skin. It is buried in the ground to ferment and dug up in the wintertime.

ᐊᖑᓇᓱᒃᑏᑦ ᑐᒃᑐᑉᐸᖕᒥᔪᑦ. ᑐᒃᑐᐃᑦ ᒪᒪᕆᓛᒃᑲ.

ᐃᓚᖏᑦ ᐊᖑᓇᓱᒃᑏᑦ ᐅᒥᐊᒃᑯᑦ ᑐᒃᑐᓯᐅᕆᐊᓲᑦ. ᐅᖅᓯᐊᖅᑎᓪᓗᒍ ᐊᐅᓪᓚᓲᑦ. ᐃᓚᖏᑦ ᓄᓇᒃᑯᑦ ᑐᒃᑐᓯᐅᕆᐊᓲᑦ, ᐊᖅᑯᑎᖅᑲᐅᖅᒪᑦ ᓴᓂᕋᔭᒃ ᐊᒥᓱᓂᒃ.

Hunters also catch caribou. Caribou meat is my favourite.

Some hunters go out on boats to find caribou. They go when the waters are calm. Others hunt caribou on land, since there are many long roads that leave Sanirajak.

ᐅᑭᐊᒃᓵᒃᑯᑦ ᓯᓚ ᓂᓪᓚᓯᙵᓂᖅᓴᐅᓕᖅᐸᒃᑐᖅ ᐊᓄᕌᒍᔨᙵᓂᖅᓴᐅᓕᖅᓱᓂᓗ. ᒪᓂᖅᑲᓗ ᐊᐱᓪᒪᓇᒃᓱᓂ. ᐅᓐᓄᒃᑯᓪᓗ ᑖᖅᓯᖅᑲᑦᑕᓕᓲᖑᓪᓗᓂ, ᐃᓄᐃᑦ ᐅᓐᓄᒃᑯᑦ ᐊᓃᙱᓐᓂᖅᓴᐅᓕᖅᑲᑦᑕᖅᑐᑦ. ᓱᓕ ᐊᓃᖅᑲᑎᒋᔭᓇᐊᖓ ᖁᕕᐊᒋᖅᑲᑦᑕᖅᑕᒃᑲ ᐃᓚᒃᑲ, ᐅᖅᑯᒃᓴᖅᓯᒪᓂᖅᓴᐅᓕᓲᖑᔮᖓ.

In the fall the weather gets colder and windier. There's even snow on the ground. It gets dark at night again, so people don't stay out as late. I still like to go outside with my family, but I have to dress in warm clothes.

ᖁᕕᐊᒋᓛᓇᒻᒥᔭᕋ ᐅᑭᐊᒃᓵᒃᑯᑦ ᐊᒻᒨᒪᔪᖅᓯᐅᖅᓱᖓ. ᑎᐱᔭᐅᓰᙳᒻᒪᑕ ᒪᓐᓂᖅᑐᐊᓘᖃᑦᑕᖅᑎᓪᓗᒍ. ᓯᓪᔭᒃᑯᑦ ᐱᓲᔭᖅᓱᖓ ᑐᓵᙳᔭᖅᓱᖓ ᒪᓐᓂᖅᐸᓚᑦᑎᔪᒥᒃ.

ᑲᔾᔮᓂᔭᕋ ᐊᒻᒨᒪᔪᖅᑕᖅᓱᖓ. ᐊᒻᒨᒪᔪᖅᑕᕈᓐᓇᖅᑐᖓ ᐅᓪᓗᓕᒫᖅ ᐅᓐᓄᐊᓕᒫᖅ! ᑖᖅᓯᔭᕌᙵᑦ, ᐃᑭᑦᑕᖅᑐᕋ ᐊᑐᖅᓱᒍ ᕿᓃᓐᓇᓰᙳᔪᖓ.

One of my favourite things to do in the fall is collecting clams. They wash up on the shoreline. I listen to the waves as I walk along the shoreline.

I love collecting clams. I could collect them all day and night! When it starts to get dark, I just pull out my flashlight and keep looking.

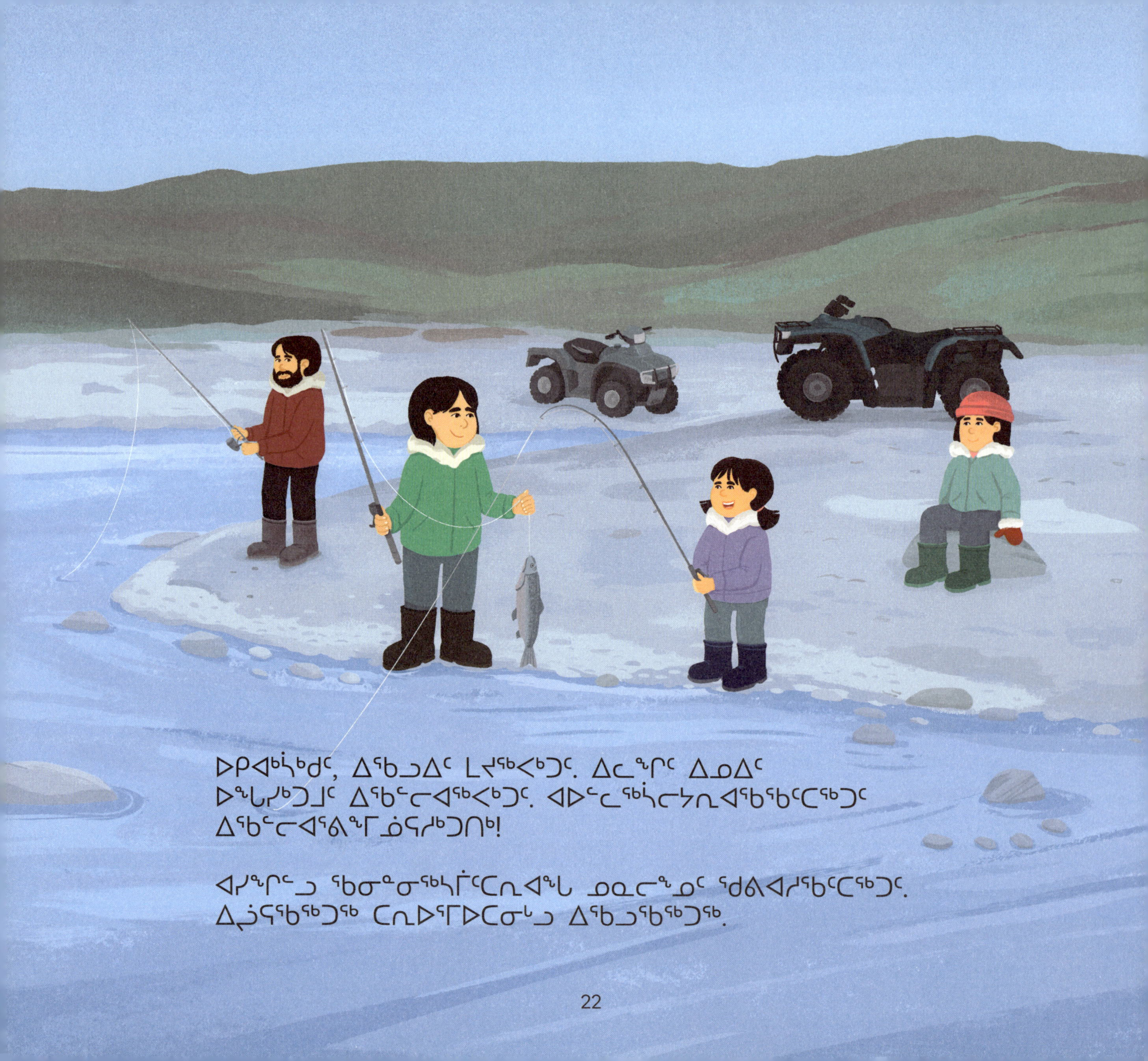

ᐅᑭᐊᒃᓵᒃᑯᑦ, ᐃᖃᓗᐃᑦ ᒪᔪᖅᐸᒃᑐᑦ. ᐃᓚᖏᑦ ᐃᓄᐃᑦ ᐅᖓᓯᒃᑐᒧᑦ ᐃᖃᓪᓕᐊᖅᐸᒃᑐᑦ. ᐊᐅᓪᓚᖅᓵᓕᔾᔪᑎᐊᖃᖃᑦᑕᖅᑐᑦ ᐃᖃᓪᓕᐊᕝᕕᖕᒥᓅᕋᓱᒃᑐᑎᒃ!

ᐊᓯᖏᓪᓗ ᖃᓂᓐᓂᖅᓴᒦᑦᑕᓇᐊᖓ ᓄᓇᓕᖕᓄᑦ ᖁᕕᐊᓱᖃᑦᑕᖅᑐᑦ. ᐃᓘᕋᖃᖅᑐᖅ ᑕᓇᐅᕐᒥᐅᑕᓂᒡᓗ ᐃᖃᓗᖃᖅᑐᖅ.

In the fall, the fish go upriver. Some people travel far to fish. They have to leave early in the day to get to their fishing spots!

Others like to stay closer and go to the lakes near our community. There are trout and char in those lakes.

ᐅᑭᐅᒃᑯᑦ ᓴᓂᕋᔭᒃ ᓂᒡᓚᔪᒃᑐᐊᓘᕗᖅ. ᖅᑲᓐᓂᖅᑲᑦᑕᓕᖅᑐᓂ,
ᓯᑯᓯᒪᓕᖅᑐᓂᓗ. ᑳᖅᓯᓴᕋᐃᖅᑲᑦᑕᓕᖅᐸᓪᓕᐊᑐᐃᓐᓇᖅᑐᓂᓗ.

ᓄᖅᑲᖕᓛᕈᑎᒋᖅᑲᑦᑕᙱᒋᑕᕗᑦ. ᐊᖕᒍᓇᓱᒃᑏᑦ ᐅᓪᓗᒐᓴᓂᒃ ᑐᒃᑐᓕᐊᖅᓯᒪᕙᒃᑐᑦ.
ᐃᓚᖕᒋᓪᓗ ᐊᖕᒍᓇᓱᒃᑏᑦ ᐳᐃᔾᓇᓱᖅᑲᑦᑕᖅᑐᑦ ᓯᓈᖕᒐᓂ.

Winters in Sanirajak are cold. It is very snowy, and the sea is covered in ice. The days get shorter and shorter.

That doesn't stop us from going outside, though. People leave for days to hunt caribou. Some hunters go to the floe edge to hunt for sea mammals.

ᐊᖑᓇᓱᒃᑏᑦ ᓴᓂᕋᔭᖕᒥ ᐊᔪᙱᑦᑐᐊᓗᐃᑦ. ᐅᐱᒋᔮᓗᒃᑲ.

ᐊᖑᓇᓱᒃᑏᑦ ᓂᕆᔭᖅᑐᖅᑰᕆᓲᑦ ᐊᖑᑕᒥᓂᒃ ᐊᕙᒃᑎᖅᑲᖅᖢᑎᒃ.
ᖁᕕᐊᒋᔮᓗᒪ ᓂᕆᖅᑕᐅᑦᑐᖓ!

Hunters in Sanirajak are very skilled. I am really proud of them.

A lot of the time, hunters invite people over to share the meat they have caught. I feel so happy when I get to join them!

ᓂᓇᖅᑲᑎᒌᖕᓂᖅ ᐃᓕᖅᑯᓯᑦᑕ ᐃᓚᒋᒻᒪᒍ. ᓄᓇᓕᖕᒥᐅᓕᒫᑦ ᐊᐅᓪᓚᕈᓐᓇᖅᑐᐃᓐᓇᐅᕙᖖᒋᒻᒪᑕ.

ᐃᓄᐃᑦ ᐅᑎᕌᖕᒐᑕ ᓴᓂᕋᔭᖕᒧᑦ, ᐊᖕᒍᑕᒥᓂᕐᒥᓂᒃ ᐊᕙᒍᓯᓲᖕᒍᕗᑦ ᓄᓇᖅᑲᑎᒥᓄᑦ. ᐊᖕᒐᔪᖅᑳᑦᑎᓐᓄᑦ ᐃᓕᓐᓂᐊᖅᑎᑕᐅᓯᒪᒐᑦᑕ ᐊᕙᒃᑯᑎᖅᑲᖅᑲᑦᑕᖅᑯᔭᐅᓪᓗᑕ ᐱᖅᑲᕌᖕᒐᑦᑕ. ᑕᒪᓐᓇ ᐱᒻᒪᕆᐊᓘᕗᖅ ᑲᔪᓯᑎᑦᑕᕆᐊᖕᒐ.

Sharing with others is part of our culture. Not everybody in our community can go out on the land.

When people return to Sanirajak, they share what they caught with people in the community. We have been taught by our parents to share when we have more than enough. It is important to pass that teaching on.

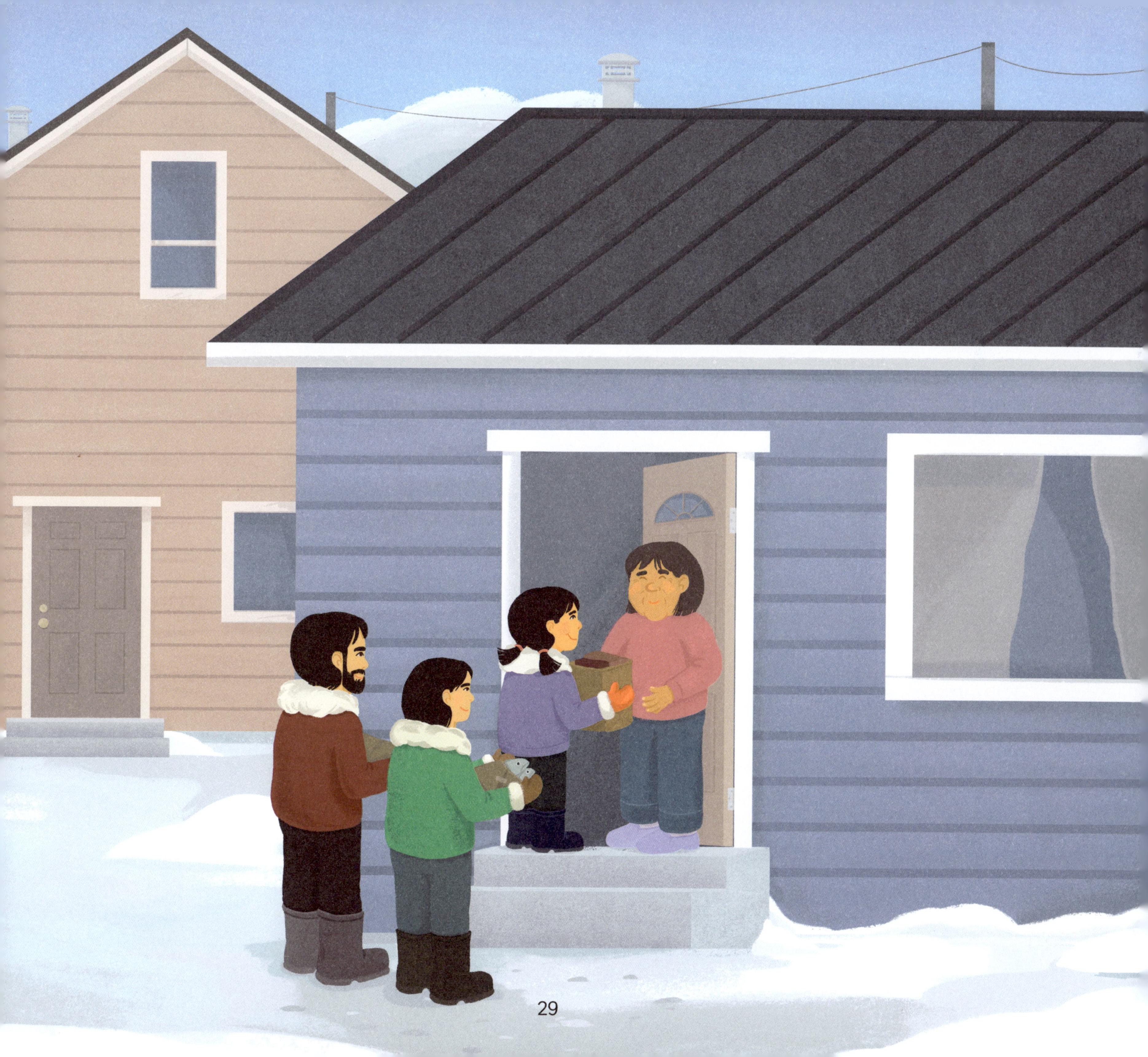

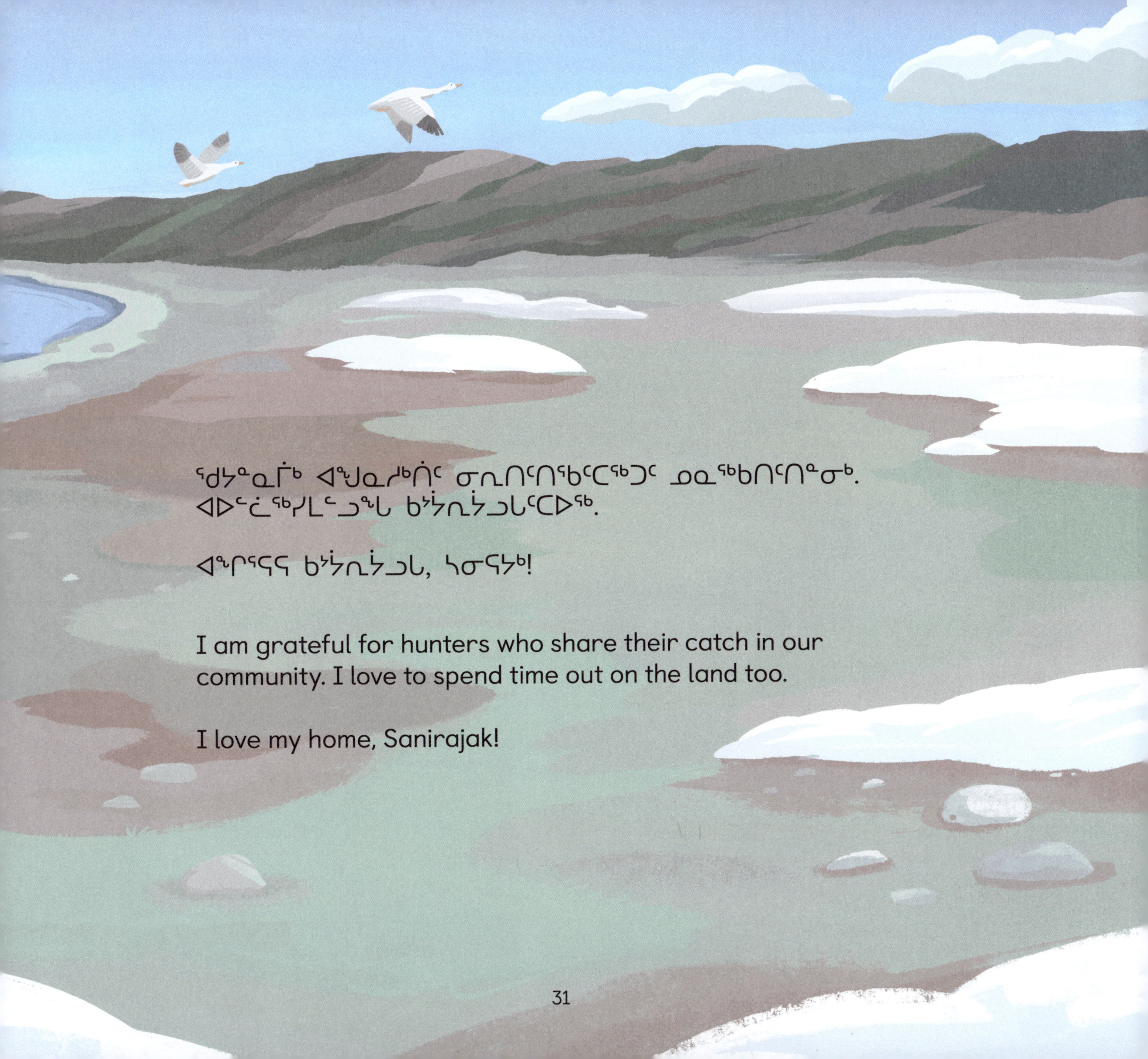

ᖁᔭᓐᓇᒦᒃ ᐊᖑᓇᓱᒃᑏᑦ ᓂᕆᑎᑦᑎᖃᑦᑕᖅᑐᑦ ᓄᓇᖅᑲᑎᑦᑎᓐᓂᒃ.
ᐊᐅᓪᓛᖅᓯᒪᓪᓗᖓ ᑲᔾᔮᕆᔾᔮᓗᒐᑦᑕᐅᖅ.

ᐊᖏᕋᕋ ᑲᔾᔮᕆᔾᔮᓗᒐ, ᓴᓂᕋᔭᒃ!

I am grateful for hunters who share their catch in our community. I love to spend time out on the land too.

I love my home, Sanirajak!

ᖃᓄᐃᓕᐅᕈᑏᑦ ᐊᖏᔪᖅᑳᕆᔭᐅᔪᓄᑦ ᐊᒻᒪᓗ ᐃᓕᓴᐃᔨᓄᑦ

Activities for Parents and Teachers

ᐅᖃᖃᑎᒌᓪᓗᒃ!

ᐊᐱᕆᖃᑦᑕᖅᐸᑕ ᓱᕈᓯᓛᑦ ᐃᓱᒪᕙᓐᓇᖅᓯᕚᓪᓕᖃᔭᖅᑐᑦ ᐅᓂᒃᑳᒥ ᐊᔾᔨᓯᕙᓐᓇᖅᓯᓗᑎᒡᓗ, ᐅᖃᕆᐅᖅᓴᖅᐸᓪᓗᑎᒃ ᐅᖃᐅᓯᖅᑕᖏᓐᓂᒃ ᐅᖅᑲᕆᒃᓯᕚᓪᓕᖃᓗᑎᒃ ᓈᓚᒍᓐᓇᖅᓯᒃᑲᓐᓂᖃᓗᑎᒡᓗ. ᐅᖃᓕᒫᕈᒃ ᓴᓂᕋᔭᒃ, ᑲᔾᔮᕆᔭᕋ. ᐅᖃᓕᒫᓕᖅᑭᓪᓗᒍ ᐊᐱᕆᓗᒋᓪᓗ ᐅᑯᓂᖓ ᐅᖃᓕᒫᖅᑎᓪᓗᑎᑦ:

- ᖃᓄᐃᓕᐅᕆᐊᖓ ᐋᓕᔅ ᖁᕕᐊᒋᔭᖅᑲᖅᐸ?
- ᐋᓕᔅ ᑭᓱᓂᒃ ᐅᐱᕐᖔᒃᑯᑦ ᓄᐊᑦᑎᕙᒃᐸ?
- ᓴᓂᕋᔭᖕᒥ ᑭᓱᓐᓇᓱᓲᖑᕙᑦ ᐊᐅᔭᒃᑯᑦ?
- ᓴᓂᕋᔭᖕᒥ ᑭᓱᓐᓇᓱᓲᖑᕙᑦ ᐅᑭᐊᒃᓵᒃᑯᑦ?
- ᓴᓂᕋᔭᖕᒥ ᑭᓱᓐᓇᓱᓲᖑᕙᑦ ᐅᑭᐅᒃᑯᑦ?
- ᓂᕿᓂᒃ ᖃᓄᐃᑦᑐᓂᒃ ᐋᓕᔅ ᒪᒪᕆᔭᖃᓛᖑᕙ?

Let's Talk!

Asking questions encourages young children to think about and connect with the story, as well as to practise using their vocabulary and speaking and listening skills. Read *Sanirajak, a Place I Love* once through. Then read the story again and ask the following questions as you read:

- What activities does Alice enjoy?
- What does Alice collect in the spring?
- What animals are hunted in the summer in Sanirajak?
- What animals are hunted in the fall in Sanirajak?
- What animals are hunted in the winter in Sanirajak?
- What type of meat is Alice's favourite?

ᐅᓂᒃᑳᓅᑦ ᑐᓴᖅᑕᐅᑎᓪᓗᒋᑦ

ᐅᑯᓂ ᐱᓕᕆᐊᒃᓴᒥ, ᓱᕈᓰᑦ ᑐᓴᖅᑕᐅᑎᑦᑎᓂᐊᖅᑐᑦ ᐊᑐᖅᓯᒪᔭᕐᒥᖕᓂᒃ ᐊᖑᓇᓱᒋᐊᖅᓯᒪᓪᓗᑎᒃ ᓄᓇᒥᑦᑐᓂᒡᔫᓐᓃᑦ ᓄᐊᑦᑎᓪᓗᑎᒃ. ᑕᐃᒪ ᑎᑎᖅᑐᒐᕐᓗᑎᒃ ᐊᑐᖅᓯᒪᔭᕐᒥᖕᓂᒃ.

ᐊᑐᐊᕐᓗᒋᑦ

1. ᐊᐱᕆᒃᑭᑦ ᓱᕈᓰᑦ ᐊᖑᓇᓱᒋᐊᓚᐅᖅᓯᒪᖕᒪᖔᑕ. ᐊᐱᕆᔪᓐᓇᕐᒥᔭᑎᑦ ᐊᖑᓇᓱᖕᓂᕐᒥᒃ ᖃᐅᔨᒪᔭᖃᕐᒪᖔᑕ, ᐊᖑᓇᓱᖕᓂᕐᒥᒃ ᐊᓂᒃᑳᓂᒃ ᑐᓴᐅᒪᔭᖃᕐᒪᖔᑕ, ᐅᓂᒃᑲᐅᓯᖃᕈᓐᓇᕐᒪᖔᑕᓗ ᐱᕈᖅᑐᓂᒃ, ᓄᓇᕋᕐᓂᒃ, ᓂᕆᔭᒃᓴᓂᒡᓗ ᑲᑎᖅᓱᐃᓲᖑᖕᒪᖔᑕ. ᑎᑎᕋᕈᒪᑐᐃᓐᓇᕆᐊᖃᖅᑕᑎᑦ ᓱᕈᓰᑦ ᑭᒡᒍᓯᖕᒋᑦ.
2. ᐃᓕᓐᓂᐊᖅᑎᑦ ᐊᐱᕆᒃᑭᑦ ᓂᕈᐊᖅᓱᕐᑯᓗᒋᑦ ᐃᖅᑲᐅᒪᔭᕐᒥᓂᒃ ᐅᓂᒃᑳᕐᒥᓂᒡᔫᓐᓃᑦ ᐅᕐᑲᒪᔭᐅᑎᕕᓂᕐᒥᒃ ᐱᐅᓪᓕᐊᓂᖅ 1. ᑕᐃᒪ ᑎᑎᖅᑐᒐᖅᑎᓪᓗᒋᑦ ᐊᑐᖅᓯᒪᔭᕐᒥᓂᒃ. ᐃᓕᓐᓂᐊᖅᑎᑦ ᐃᖅᑲᐅᒪᓇᓱᕐᑯᒃᑭᑦ ᑕᑯᓐᓇᙱᐊᕐᑯᓗᒋᓪᓗ ᖃᓄᐃᑦᑑᓂᖏᓐᓂᒃ ᓯᓚᐅᑉ ᐊᓯᔾᔨᖅᑕᕐᓂᖏᓐᓂᒃ, ᑕᖅᓴᖏᓐᓂᒃ, ᐱᕈᖅᑐᓂᒃ, ᐆᒪᔪᓂᒡᓗ ᑕᑯᔭᕕᓂᕐᒥᒃ, ᐊᓯᖏᓐᓂᒡᓗ.
3. ᐃᓕᓐᓂᐊᖅᑎᑦ ᐅᖃᓪᓚᐅᑎᖃᖅᑎᒃᑭᑦ ᑎᑎᖅᑐᒐᖅᑕᒥᖕᓂᒃ. ᐊᐱᕆᒃᑭᑦ ᖃᓄᖅ ᐃᒃᐱᒍᓱᖕᒪᖔᑕ ᐊᔾᔨᙳᐊᓕᐊᖏᓐᓂᒃ ᖃᓄᕐᓗ ᐊᔾᔨᖃᕐᓗᖕᒪᖔᑕ ᐊᔾᔨᙵᖏᓪᓗᖕᒪᖔᑕᓗ ᓴᓂᕋᔭᒃ, ᑲᔾᔮᓇᔭᕋ.

Sharing Our Stories

In this activity, children will share their personal experiences of hunting or collecting things from the land. Then they will each draw a picture based on their experiences.

Directions

1. Ask the children if they have ever gone hunting. You could also ask what they know about hunting, if they have heard any hunting stories, or if they have stories about collecting plants, flowers, or herbs. You may choose to write down the children's answers.
2. Ask the children to choose a memory or a story from the discussion in step 1. Then have them each draw a picture of their experience. Encourage the children to remember or imagine details such as the season, the colours around them, the plants or animals they saw, and so on.
3. Have the children talk about their drawings. Ask them how their pictures make them feel and how they are similar to or different from *Sanirajak, a Place I Love.*

ᑲᑎᖅᓱᐃᓂᖅ ᓴᓂᕋᔭᐅᑉ ᐆᒪᔪᕐᒋᓐᓂᒃ

ᑕᐅᕙᓂ ᐱᓕᕆᐊᒃᓴᒥ, ᓱᕈᓰᑦ ᖃᐅᔨᒪᔭᕐᒥᓂᒃ ᐊᑐᕐᓂᐊᖅᑐᑦ ᓴᓂᕋᔭᒃ, ᑳᔅᓵᓇᔭᕋ ᐆᒪᔪᓂᒃ ᐊᖑᓇᓱᒃᑕᐅᓲᓂᒃ ᓴᓂᕋᔭᕐᒥ.

ᐊᑐᐊᕐᓗᑎᑦ

1. ᑐᖅᑯᕈᒃ ᓴᖅᑭᑎᓪᓗᒍᓗ ᑲᑎᖅᓱᐃᔾᔪᑎ ᓴᓂᕋᔭᕐᒥ ᐆᒪᔪᙳᐊᓂᒃ ᐱᓕᕆᔾᔪᑎ ᐅᕙᙵᑦ **www.arvaaq.com**.
2. ᐃᓕᓐᓂᐊᖅᑎᑦ ᐊᒥᐊᕆᑎᒃᑭᑦ ᐆᒪᔪᙳᐊᓂᒃ ᑭᐸᒌᕆᒃᑐᒦᑦᑐᓂᒃ ᑭᖑᓂᐊᒍᑦ ᐅᑭᑎᕆᓕᕐᓗᑎᒃ. (ᐃᑲᔪᕐᓗᒋᑦ ᐃᑲᔪᕆᐊᖅᑲᖅᐸᑕ.)
3. ᑕᑯᑎᒃᑭᑦ ᓱᕈᓰᑦ ᐊᔾᔨᙳᐊᓂᒃ ᐆᒪᔪᙳᐊᓂᒃ ᐅᖃᓕᒫᒐᕐᒦᑦᑐᓂᒃ ᓴᓂᕋᔭᒃ, ᑳᔅᓵᓇᔭᕋᒥ.
4. ᐃᓕᓐᓂᐊᖅᑏᑦ ᐊᔾᔨᒌᓕᖅᓱᐃᑎᒃᑭᑦ ᐆᒪᔪᙳᐊᓂᒃ ᐊᒻᒧᖓᑦᓯᓂ ᓇᓗᓇᐃᖅᑐᐃᔾᔪᓯᒥ. ᐊᒻᒧᖓᑦᓯᑦ ᑕᑯᒃᓴᐅᑎᑦᑎᔪᑦ ᓯᓚᐅᑉ ᐊᓯᔾᔨᖅᑕᕐᓂᕐᒋᓐᓂᒃ. ᐃᓕᓐᓂᐊᖅᑎᑦ ᐊᔾᔨᒌᓕᖅᓱᐃᓂᐊᖅᑐᑦ ᐆᒪᔪᙳᐊᓂ ᓯᓚᐅᑉ ᐊᓯᔾᔨᖅᑕᕐᓂᕐᒋᓐᓂᒃ ᐊᖑᓇᓱᒃᑕᐅᓲᓂᒃ ᓴᓂᕋᔭᕐᒥ.
5. ᐃᓕᓐᓂᐊᖅᑎᑦ ᓇᓗᓇᐃᖅᐸᑕ ᓇᒧᑦ ᐃᓕᓯᓂᐊᕐᒪᖔᑕ ᓇᓗᓇᐃᖅᑐᐃᔾᔪᓯᒥ, ᓂᐱᑎᑎᒃᑭᑦ ᑭᐸᒌᕆᒃᑐᖓᑦ ᐊᒻᒧᖓᑦᓱᖓᑦ ᑕᒻᒪᙵᕆᓪᓗᑎᒃ. (ᐃᑲᔪᕆᐊᖅᑲᖅᐸᑕ ᐃᑲᔪᕐᓗᒋᑦ.)
6. ᐃᓕᓐᓂᐊᖅᑎᑦ ᐆᒪᔫᑉ ᐊᑎᖏᓐᓂᒃ ᐊᑖᒍᑦ ᑎᑎᕋᖅᑯᒃᑭᑦ ᐊᔾᔨᙳᐊᖏᑕ ᑕᐃᒪᐃᑦᑐᓐᓇᖅᐸᑕ.
7. ᐱᔪᒪᑉᐸᑕ: ᐅᖃᓪᓚᐅᑎᖃᕐᓗᓯ ᐅᑭᐅᖅᑕᖅᑐᒥᐅᑕᓂᒃ ᐆᒪᔪᓂᒃ, ᖃᖓᒃᑯᑦ ᐊᖑᓇᓱᒃᑕᐅᓲᖑᒻᒪᖔᑕ ᐆᒪᔪᑦ, ᓱᕈᓰᓪᓗ ᐱᖃᑕᐅᓚᐅᖅᓯᒪᙱᒪᖔᑕ ᐊᖑᓇᓱᒃᑐᓂᒃ.

Sorting Sanirajak Animals

In this worksheet, children will have an opportunity to apply their knowledge from *Sanirajak, a Place I Love* about when animals are hunted in Sanirajak.

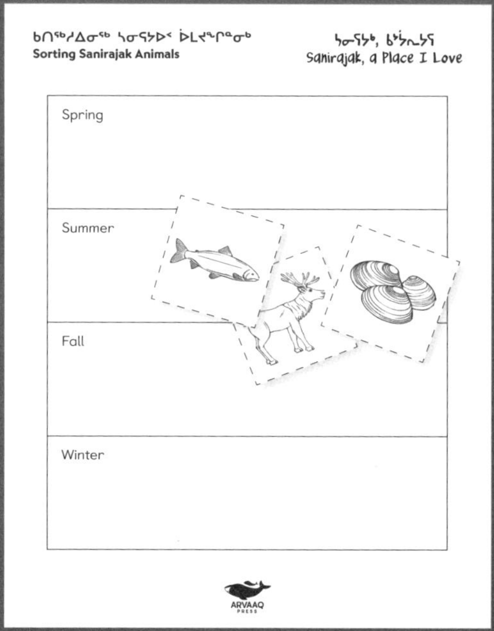

Directions

1. Download and print the Sorting Sanirajak Animals worksheets from **www.arvaaq.com**.
2. Have the children colour the animals in the squares and then cut out the squares. (Assist as needed.)
3. Show the children the pictures of the animals in the book *Sanirajak, a Place I Love.*
4. Have the children match the animals to the columns on the chart. Each column represents a season. The children will match each animal to the season it is usually hunted in Sanirajak.
5. Once the children have decided where they would like to place the animals on the chart, have them glue the squares to the correct columns. (Assist as needed.)
6. Encourage the children to write the name of each animal under each image if they are able to do so.
7. Optional: talk about other animals that live in the Arctic, when these animals are usually hunted, and if the children have experience being a part of these hunting traditions.